ENDANGERED ZEBRAS

Kelley MacAulay & Bobbie Kalman

 Crabtree Publishing Company

www.crabtreebooks.com

Earth's Endangered Animals Series
A Bobbie Kalman Book

Dedicated by Kelley MacAulay
For my beautiful niece, Kate MacAulay, who's so very loved

Editor-in-Chief
Bobbie Kalman

Writing team
Kelley MacAulay
Bobbie Kalman

Substantive editor
Kathryn Smithyman

Editors
Molly Aloian
Michael Hodge
Robin Johnson
Rebecca Sjonger

Photo research
Crystal Foxton

Design
Katherine Kantor
Margaret Amy Salter (cover)

Production coordinator
Heather Fitzpatrick

Consultant
Patricia Loesche, Ph.D., Animal Behavior Program,
Department of Psychology, University of Washington

Illustrations
Barbara Bedell: page 8
Katherine Kantor: back cover, pages 15, 26, 30
Jeannette McNaughton-Julich: page 11 (bottom)
Margaret Amy Salter: pages 7, 11 (top)

Photographs
Alpha Presse: Martin Harvey/Peter Arnold: pages 10-11, 12; Frans Lemmens/Lineair: page 29
Associated Press: page 28
ardea.com: Peter Steyn: front cover, page 9
BigStockPhoto.com: © Darren Baker: page 14; © Nico Smit: page 20
Bruce Coleman Inc.: Joseph Van Wormer: page 8
Corbis: © Bojan Brecelj: page 22; © Earl & Nazima Kowall: pages 26-27; © David Reed: page 24
Fotolia.com: © Jean François Lefevre: page 30 (top)
iStockphoto.com: Klaas Lingbeek-Van Kranen: page 25
NHPA/Photoshot: Gerald Cubitt: page 13; Martin Harvey: page 23
Photo Researchers, Inc.: Christophe Ratier: page 17
© ShutterStock.com/SouWest Photography: pages 1, 31
Visuals Unlimited: Gerald & Buff Corsi: page 18
Other images by Adobe Image Library, Digital Stock, Digital Vision, Iconotec, and Photodisc

Library and Archives Canada Cataloguing in Publication

MacAulay, Kelley
    Endangered zebras / Kelley MacAulay & Bobbie Kalman.

(Earth's endangered animals)
Includes index.
ISBN 978-0-7787-1864-2 (bound)
ISBN 978-0-7787-1910-6 (pbk.)

    1. Zebras--Juvenile literature. 2. Endangered species--Juvenile
literature. I. Kalman, Bobbie, 1947- II. Title. III. Series.

QL737.U62M33 2007   j599.665'7   C2007-900530-6

Library of Congress Cataloging-in-Publication Data

MacAulay, Kelley.
    Endangered zebras / Kelley MacAulay & Bobbie Kalman.
      p. cm. -- (Earth's endangered animals)
    Includes index.
    ISBN-13: 978-0-7787-1864-2 (rlb)
    ISBN-10: 0-7787-1864-6 (rlb)
    ISBN-13: 978-0-7787-1910-6 (pb)
    ISBN-10: 0-7787-1910-3 (pb)
    1. Zebras--Juvenile literature. 2. Endangered species--Juvenile literature.
I. Kalman, Bobbie. II. Title. III. Series.
    QL737.U62M24 2007
    599.665'7--dc22

2007002690

Crabtree Publishing Company
www.crabtreebooks.com   1-800-387-7650

Published in Canada
Crabtree Publishing
616 Welland Ave.
St. Catharines, ON
L2M 5V6

Published in the United States
Crabtree Publishing
PMB16A
350 Fifth Ave., Suite 3308
New York, NY 10118

Published in the United Kingdom
Crabtree Publishing
White Cross Mills
High Town, Lancaster
LA1 4XS

Published in Australia
Crabtree Publishing
386 Mt. Alexander Rd.
Ascot Vale (Melbourne)
VIC 3032

Contents

Endangered!

Thousands of animals on Earth are **endangered**. Endangered animals are at risk of dying out in the **wild**, or in the natural places not controlled by people. Two of the three main groups of zebras are endangered. People must try to save zebras, or all zebras may become **extinct**.

Words to know

Scientists use certain words to describe animals that are in danger. Some of these words are listed below.

vulnerable Describes animals that may soon become endangered

endangered Describes animals that are in danger of dying out in the wild

critically endangered Describes animals that are at high risk of dying out in the wild

extinct Describes animals that are no longer known to live anywhere on Earth

4

What are zebras?

Zebras are **mammals**. Mammals are animals that have backbones. They are also **warm-blooded**. Most mammals have hair or fur on their bodies. Baby mammals **nurse**, or drink milk from the bodies of their mothers.

The Equidae family

Zebras belong to the **Equidae family**. Horses and asses also belong to this family. Most of the animals in the Equidae family live in groups called **herds**. Zebras live in herds.

Three groups

The three main groups of zebras are mountain zebras, Grévy's zebras, and plains zebras. Mountain zebras and Grévy's zebras are endangered.

Plains zebras are also known as common zebras or Burchell's zebras. Plains zebras are not endangered. The number of plains zebras living in the wild is dropping, however.

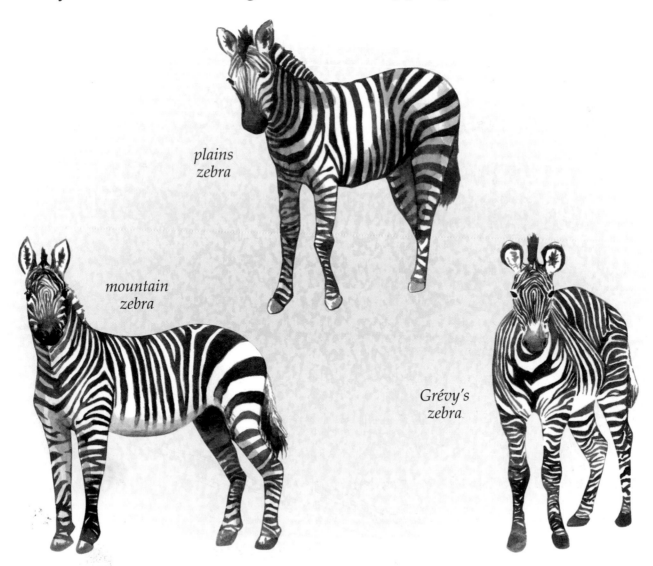

plains zebra

mountain zebra

Grévy's zebra

7

Where do zebras live?

Zebras live in Africa, which is one of the hottest places on Earth! Different zebras live in different African **habitats**. A habitat is the natural place where an animal lives.

Plains zebra habitats

Plains zebras are found throughout most of southeast Africa. They live in **savanna** and **open woodland** habitats. Savannas are wide, flat areas of land. They are covered with grasses and a few trees. Open woodlands are areas with scattered trees.

Grévy's zebra habitats

Most Grévy's zebras live in northern Kenya. They live in **semi-desert** habitats. **Deserts** are dry places.

Semi-desert habitats are also dry but patches of grasses grow there. Most semi-desert habitats are between deserts and savannas.

Mountain zebra habitats

Most mountain zebras live in habitats on mountains. Some mountain zebras live in savannas and open woodlands in South Africa. Other mountain zebras live in semi-desert habitats near the Namib Desert.

This mountain zebra lives in a savanna habitat.

Zebra bodies

All zebras look similar. They have short, soft fur covering their bodies. Zebras are well known for the black-and-white-striped patterns of their fur. Different groups of zebras have slightly different bodies, however. Mountain zebras are the smallest and lightest zebras. Grévy's zebras are the largest and heaviest zebras. Grévy's zebras also have bigger ears and longer heads than plains zebras and mountain zebras have.

Every zebra has a different pattern of stripes on its body.

A zebra has strong legs for running. It can run up to 35 miles (56 km) per hour!

10

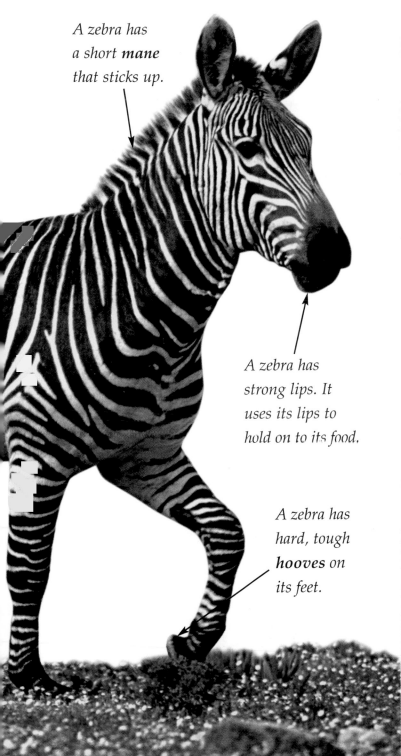

*A zebra has a short **mane** that sticks up.*

A zebra has strong lips. It uses its lips to hold on to its food.

*A zebra has hard, tough **hooves** on its feet.*

So stripy!

The easiest way to tell the three groups of zebras apart is by looking at their stripes. Plains zebras have wide **vertical** stripes on the front halves of their bodies. The stripes on the back halves of their bodies and on their legs are **horizontal**. Grévy's zebra stripes are similar to those of plains zebras, but they are thinner and more evenly spaced. Mountain zebras, such as the one shown left, have narrow stripes at the front of their bodies. They have wider stripes on their rear ends.

plains zebra

Grévy's zebra

Finding food and water

Herbivores are animals that eat only plants. Zebras are herbivores. They eat mainly grasses. They snip off grasses using their sharp **incisors**, or front teeth. They then chew the food using their flat back teeth. Zebras sometimes eat roots and **bulbs**, which they dig up from the ground using their hooves.

Zebras pull the food into their mouths using their strong lips.

Grazing on grasses

Grasses have few **nutrients**. Zebras must eat a lot of grasses to get the nutrients they need to survive. Zebras may **graze** for up to eighteen hours a day!

This mountain zebra is grazing.

12

Thirsty zebras

Zebras can live without water for a few days, but they drink every day if water is available. Zebras pick grazing spots that are near **water holes** or rivers. In very hot weather, the water in water holes and rivers sometimes dries up. Using their hooves, zebras dig into the dry ground where the water used to be. They dig down until they find water deep in the ground.

These mountain zebras are standing in a dry water hole. They will have to dig deep for water.

13

From foal to adult

Every animal goes through a set of changes from the time it is born to the time it is an adult. This set of changes is called a **life cycle**. A zebra's life cycle begins inside its mother's body. After it is born, a baby zebra is called a **foal**. A male foal is called a **colt**, and a female foal is called a **filly**. A foal grows and changes until it is **mature**, or an adult. An adult zebra can **mate**, or join together with another zebra from the same group to make babies of its own.

Imprinting

As soon as a foal is born, it forms a close **bond** with the animal that is nearest to it. The foal follows the animal with which it bonds. Forming a bond is called **imprinting**. Imprinting keeps foals close to their mothers, where they are safer from **predators**. For the first few weeks of her foal's life, a mother zebra chases away any zebra that comes close to her foal. By chasing away other zebras, the mother makes sure that her baby forms a bond only with her.

A zebra's life cycle

A mother zebra has only one foal at a time. After the foal is born, it stays close to its mother for one to three years. The foal then leaves its mother's herd and goes to live with another herd.

A colt becomes mature when it is five to six years old. A filly becomes mature when it is about a year-and-a-half old. Most mature females do not have their first foals until they are between two and five years old, however.

*When a male zebra becomes mature, it is called a **stallion**. A mature female zebra is called a **mare**.*

Most newborn zebras have brown stripes. A newborn foal can stand minutes after it is born.

As a foal grows, it spends a lot of time playing with other foals. Play helps a foal become strong enough to keep up with the herd. By the time it is a year old, the foal's stripes have turned black.

A foal nurses often during the first few months of its life. It begins to nibble at grasses when it is only a few days old, however. At about ten months old, the foal stops nursing and eats only grasses.

15

Herds called harems

The mares that have been in a harem the longest are the first mares that drink at a water hole.

Plains zebras and mountain zebras live in herds called **harems**. A harem of zebras is made up of one stallion, several mares, and several foals. Plains zebra harems usually include one stallion, about six females, and their young. Mountain zebra harems often have fewer mares than plains zebra harems do.

Leader of the pack

The stallion is a harem's leader. He protects the mares and foals from predators. The mares that have been in the harem the longest are the most important mares. They are given special treatment by the other mares. For example, they get to eat the tastiest grasses. The mares in a harem form close bonds. They often stay together for life.

Bachelor groups

When plains or mountain zebra colts are old enough to leave their mothers' harems, they live in herds called **bachelor groups**. Bachelor groups are made up of male zebras that do not have harems. The colts live in bachelor groups until they become mature stallions. Each stallion then leaves its bachelor group to form its own harem.

Smaller harems

When a filly leaves its mother's harem, it often joins a harem that is smaller than the size of its mother's harem. In a smaller harem, the filly can get more food. With fewer zebras around, each zebra gets more to eat! Also, there are fewer females in smaller harems. A mature filly in a small harem has a better chance of mating with the stallion.

Young stallions sometimes try to take over the harems of older stallions. To take over a harem, a younger stallion challenges an older stallion to a fight. If the younger stallion wins the fight, it takes over the harem. Young stallions very rarely win these fights, however.

Loose groups

Grévy's zebras live in dry areas where grasses grow mainly in scattered patches. The zebras must walk long distances to find food. Grévy's zebra mares do not form close bonds with one another because they must compete for the patches of grasses. Since the mares do not form close bonds, Grévy's zebras do not live in harems. Sometimes Grévy's zebras form **loose groups**, such as the group shown above. The members of loose groups change often. Some loose groups are made up of stallions. Others are made up of mares and their foals.

18

Living alone

Many Grévy's zebra stallions live alone in large **territories**, or areas of land. Their territories can be up to four square miles (10 km²) in size. The stallions search for territories with plenty of grasses. A territory with plenty of grasses attracts Grévy's zebra mares. When a mare enters the territory to graze, she may mate with the stallion that has claimed the territory.

Crossing the line

A Grévy's zebra stallion marks the **boundaries**, or edges, of its territory with its **dung**, or waste. When another stallion smells the dung, it knows the area already belongs to a stallion. A stallion may enter the territory of another stallion as long as the visiting stallion does not try to mate with a mare that is grazing in the territory. If it does, the stallion that marked the territory will fight the visiting stallion.

Zebra behavior

Zebras **communicate**, or send messages to one another, using sounds. A zebra makes a soft sound called a **whinny** to find another zebra in a group. Mother zebras whinny to tell their foals to come close. Zebras make loud squealing sounds when they see predators or when they are hurt. Zebras also communicate by making faces. For example, an angry zebra opens its mouth and points back its ears.

*Zebras often take **dust baths** by rolling in dust, as this mountain zebra is doing. The dust helps protect a zebra's body from biting insects.*

20

Good grooming

Zebras nibble one another's fur in order to **groom**, or clean, their bodies. Grooming removes dirt and insects from the bodies of the zebras and gives itchy zebras a nice scratch! Grooming also helps zebras form bonds. Mares in harems groom one another often. Mother zebras also groom their foals often.

Always alert

Zebras must always watch for predators that are nearby. Zebra predators include lions, cheetahs, leopards, hyenas, and crocodiles. In zebra herds, one zebra watches for predators at all times. For example, while the herd sleeps at night, one zebra stays awake, on the lookout for predators.

Zebras watch for predators even while grooming one another! When two zebras are grooming, they face in opposite directions so that each zebra can guard for predators.

Losing their lands

Habitat loss is one of the main threats that zebras face in the wild. Habitat loss is the destruction of natural habitats by people. The number of people in Africa is growing quickly. The people need food and homes. Each year, they **clear** huge areas of zebra habitats.

To clear is to remove all the plants from an area. People clear the land to create space to plant **crops** and to build new homes. Crops are plants that people grow for food. When their habitats are cleared, zebras have nowhere to live and no food to eat.

This land was once a zebra habitat. People are burning the plants on the land to clear them away. They will then plant crops on the land.

Tough competition

Many farmers in Africa raise **livestock**. Livestock are animals, such as cows, which people raise for food. Livestock eat the same grasses that zebras eat, so people place huge herds of livestock in zebra habitats. Like zebras, the livestock need to eat a lot of plants to get the nutrients they need. When livestock graze in zebra habitats, zebra herds do not get enough food to eat, causing many zebras to starve.

A large part of this zebra habitat has been fenced off to allow the livestock to graze.

Water woes

These livestock are drinking at a water hole in a zebra habitat. Many animals have to share the small amount of water that is available.

Livestock also drink at water holes and from rivers in zebra habitats. During a **drought**, there is only a little water available, but there are a lot of animals that need to drink. When livestock drink at the water holes in zebra habitats, many zebras do not get enough water. Some zebras die from **dehydration**, or lack of water.

Fenced out

Some farmers build fences around the water holes in zebra habitats. The farmers build the fences so that only their livestock can drink the water. The fences prevent zebras from reaching the water they need to stay alive.

A hot topic

Global warming also harms zebras and their habitats. Global warming is the gradual rise in temperatures on Earth. Around the world, people burn huge amounts of fuels such as coal, oil, and gas. People burn these fuels to heat their homes, to run their cars, and to get electricity. Many scientists believe that burning these fuels adds to global warming. As the temperature gets hotter in Africa, water holes and rivers in zebra habitats dry up for longer and longer periods of time. Without water, many zebras die from dehydration.

This zebra foal died from dehydration.

Hunting zebras

In the past, hunters killed thousands of zebras for their skins. Zebra skins were used to make rugs, coats, purses, slippers, and wall hangings. Today, it is **illegal**, or against the law, to hunt endangered zebras. Some people continue to kill zebras illegally, however. The picture on the right shows the skins of recently killed zebras.

Today, many endangered zebras live on **preserves**. Preserves are natural areas where animals are protected by governments. Many zebras live on preserves in their natural habitats.

Safe zebras

On preserves, zebras are protected from habitat loss and hunting. They also do not have to compete with livestock for food and water. **Rangers** are people who patrol preserves to keep animals safe from people who hunt zebras illegally. Scientists on preserves study zebras to find out what they need to survive in their habitats.

Veterinarians work on preserves. Veterinarians are doctors who treat animals. This veterinarian is treating a sick zebra foal. He is giving the foal the medicine it needs to survive.

Getting people involved

Many **conservation groups** are working to save zebras. Conservation groups are groups of people who protect animals and their habitats. One way conservation groups help zebras is by getting local people involved in zebra research. For example, in Kenya, one conservation group has created the Grévy's Zebra Scout Program.

This program hires people from local communities to research Grévy's zebras in the wild. The people watch zebras and write down how many zebras they see and where the zebras are living. This program helps scientists learn about Grévy's zebras and also helps the local people earn money.

This man has been hired to research zebras that live near his community.

Helping out

You can help zebras by learning about them and then sharing what you know with others. There are many places where you can learn more about zebras. Visit your local library to read other books. The library may even have DVDs about zebras that you can borrow!

A

B

The Internet

You can also find information about zebras on the Internet. Begin by checking out this website:

www.panda.org/news_facts/education/middle_school/
species/herbivores/zebra/index.cfm

Which is which?

Did you know that scientists are not sure why zebras have stripes? Some scientists believe that zebras learn the stripe patterns of the zebras with which they like to spend time. The zebras then use the different stripe patterns to recognize one another in a herd. Can you tell which zebra group is which by looking at their stripe patterns? Look at the zebras on these pages and decide which zebra belongs to which group. For hints, re-read the box called "So Stripy!" on page eleven.

C

Answers: A: Grévy's zebra   B: plains zebras   C: mountain zebra

Glossary

Note: Boldfaced words that are defined in the text may not appear in the glossary.

bond Caring feelings between zebras

bulb The round underground parts of some plants

desert A hot, dry area that receives less than ten inches (25 cm) of rain each year

drought A period of time during which little rain falls

Equidae family A family of mammals that includes zebras, horses, and asses

graze To eat grasses

horizontal Describing something that is straight across

loose group A group of animals whose members change often

nutrients Substances that animals need to grow and to stay healthy

predator An animal that hunts and eats other animals

rangers People who work on preserves to protect the animals that live there

vertical Describing something that is straight up and down

warm-blooded Describing animals that have body temperatures that stay about the same, no matter how hot or cold their surroundings are

water hole A natural pool where water collects and to which animals go to drink and bathe

wild Describes natural places that are not controlled by people

Index

Printed in the U.S.A.